.

FIFTY-SIX

FIFTY SIX

a poem sequence by

George Szirtes
& Carol Watts

2016

Published by Arc Publications,
Nanholme Mill, Shaw Wood Road
Todmorden OL14 6DA, UK
www.arcpublications.co.uk

Copyright in the poems
© George Szirtes & Carol Watts, 2016
(as indicated)
Copyright in the present edition © Arc Publications 2016

978 1910345 11 5 (pbk)
978 1910345 12 2 (hbk)
978 1910345 13 9 (ebk)

Design by Tony Ward
Cover design by Tony Ward & Ben Styles
Printed in Great Britain by
TJ International, Padstow, Cornwall

ACKNOWLEDGEMENTS
The first 28 verses appeared in
the *Long Poem Magazine* Issue 10, October 2013

This book is in copyright. Subject to statutory exception and to
provision of relevant collective licensing agreements,
no reproduction of any part of this book may take place
without the written permission of Arc Publications.

**Editor for the UK and Ireland:
John W. Clarke**

AUTHORS' NOTE

Collaboration at its best is a magical form of encounter, a curious listening and discovery. There is sometimes a vertiginous feeling in this exchange, meeting the way another poet thinks and inhabits the process of writing, with habits and unspoken intensities of your own. This negotiation is unpredictable, and exhilarating. There's play and resistance. Feet find different ground. New forms emerge.

The 56 poems in this collection began with a meeting instigated by S. J. Fowler as part of his Camarade project, in which poets of different sorts and temperaments were encouraged to work with each other, each pair finding their own method of collaboration.

We had not met before, and began by reading each other's poetry. A single poem of 28 lines started the process, in which Carol responded to a painting from Jenny Saville's *Red Stare* series, withholding that information from George. Like a secret ekphrasis, wondering how the material might be picked up to go on a journey. George responded with a poem of 27 lines, and the trajectory seemed clear. Each poem would be one line shorter than the last until the theme was stripped down to one line alone. The collaboration took on a life and pace of its own, and we worked back to 28 lines again, 56 poems in all.

The exchange became much more than a collaborative game for both of us. In a process of speaking-singing Chaucer surfaced, a whaling song, fragments of overheard conversation, the thickness of paint. What fields of lyricism open up under the circumstances? What might be freed and explored further? We became involved less in the mechanism, more in the rich ground that kept opening. The exchange is littered with fractures and hints, with associations that leap off in both linguistic and narrative directions. The whole is about loving language and things equally, almost interchangeably. There is childhood, fragility, sleep and waking in it, the turn of a year. And a thread throughout, of a child coming to language in a damaged world. A fragment thieved by Carol from George's poetry produced a turning point. 'What else to take from a mouth's / exception'. The stakes of song, perhaps, in 56 poems. And the number 56, itself suddenly talismanic, the year when George came to these shores.

George Szirtes & Carol Watts

FIFTY-SIX

1

Are you savant, that flesh comes to you
named in colours, beautiful & impasto.
Tell me it isn't tragic, when light descends
on newest skin, the curl of a neck.
What is the colour I can't say, breaking
through the face, where time renders it.
Wide as reclaimed land, spilt rain.
Is it solace that finds you rose. Or
waking with it, a shepherd's warning
shifts you along, knowing you alive yet
slipt into something wholly abstract.
Don't go there, stay. This flesh is warm &
marked in parturition, the face gives way
to harm, its weight is red. Red is this day
corrosion, where blush would be acting on.
What is taken away, or begins expelling
in the soft paleness, where minutes pass.
Not suffused, but colour stripped from
worldliness, an outside worn on skin,
life abrasions. Barriers give way to.
Rust & inundation. For now you are a child.
You have not seen this colour. Remain
unknowing in larger scale, bold &
meticulous. In your red stare, life moves
fast, words are outflung birds, colour
without capture. But flesh binds you
tight to palette, builds its fens & ochres,
your pink wash & plasmas weep it.

[CW]

2

Don't go there, stay, where the hand moves through
the delicate closures of the spectrum, which is
now flesh now water now a compound of shadow
and accident. The terrace exposed, the cranium
alight with hair, hat, awning, breeze – all obscurities.
If birth were language, if the clear and icy blue
of the imagination could be named. The eye speaks
its own tongue, understands its own idiolect,
its patois of slurs and blindings, knows how to follow
a moving dot, recognises rose, thrift, geranium,
and all the dustings of grass. The pram curls around
the child as if it were nature on a mission to protect
its stranger productions. What we seal in language breaks
open in front of us, the very idea of us broken
into leaves, molecules, atoms. We are broken down
into these infinitesimal spots of light and sound.
Listen: wings, winds, blinds, pinks, mornings, rain
with its caesuras. Something is focusing then gone.
Gone again. But we like it, meaning you and I and we
in our aspects of liking. It is, isn't it, as if we could drown
in gestures of liking. Too much, then again too much.
Too much of gesture and of words but not enough
of colour or terrace or awning or child, of the rough
hand about its business, of the thought of the sea
at the back of the head, of nothing and no one.
This, we say, is a spectrum. This is what we may clutch
and abandon. And we know not to stay there. We go.

[GS]

3

She remains, or. There is silence her side
of facehood, coming in to speech.
Might it be a roar, or in attenuation
a thread clutched on to. We: a future
conflagration, its shadows light her face,
a glow, a burn. Language tries to seal,
but it is a raw thing, in truth. Coming
to her lips. Her eyes know where pity is,
adult shame, lives lost, complicity with
what is out of reach & nonetheless a naming.
All else is translation, & there again,
a strangeness of arriving. Birth
marked, is a red stain bursting from a pod,
is broadcast. Her face can't escape it, eyes
water, though skin resolves to the right.
Becomes colour of paper, blanched free to.
Compromise. Which is the closer lived.
Sheen of. Planes of attention, knowing
herself watched. Why is she of consequence
to this older gaze & its dehiscence. Hers is
keener, a mackerel shoal disaggregating
crosses skin, sounds of shouts & speed.
Streamlines entering into the thought she is.
Would be blue & silver, with deeper bruise
running gauntlets, murmurate, plunging into
flight. Does she run to sound.

[CW]

4

All else is translation. Thus and thus and thus.
Dustings. *Korpa*. Dead skin. Dehiscence.
The his-sense. It is the breaking
down into phonemes   of colour
spectra, specked Ra, specked tra-la…
      See, you move and you move
and stay still. That is
translation. One speaks, so to say, trans-
lationally. Rawly of raw things. Of lips
synching sound, sunk, lipsunk. Every speck
goes missing. Every speck is a pointilliste
gesture. Every speck-tra-la. Look, here is a head
on a lap, here is a head between palms, here
is a voice we have suddenly recognised,
emerging from its camouflage, its natural
colouring blended, bladed, bled into corres-
pondence. He does not speak, he parses.
It passes through puns and penury
into this form of speech. Into what remains,
into the remainders, the remnants, the re-
monstrances, into the monstrous that slips
like all slippages, out of the core
into its own marginalia, its reimagining
into the perpetual hover between desire
and its objects, into its own remaining.

[GS]

5

Perpetual hover, what breaks into clear
lichor, runs from open. Blasts & clots,
refusing binding. Stays wet for days, posed
for medical magazines. Flushed through
crimson, spread as thin as. Flight, taking
off through branches. Each a possible
movement, without investigation, line of
trees, switched in shuddered time lapse.
Tissue factors, begin swarm, held in full
suspension, are crimson, but words swim
straw & coagulate. She runs to loosen, or
blot. There are starling forces, building
across her face, needing universal donors:
sit down why don't you. Watch the slippage,
it waits close by to catch you gazing. Wet
stuff on the face, turns to drizzle in late
morning, clouds. While the roof gives way
to missiles, small sons. Lost to armies,
try speech. Out, who did this. Her image
is removed from supermarkets against a
blue background. Perhaps there is no sound
here. I would parse it while it knits, prompt her.
From the mark she wears, still wet on the wall,
still heavier with flesh & beginning.

[CW]

6

And then she... and then the child, the magazine,
the shops, the rain. Still heavier with beginning,
     gravities of footfall and knittage, the shapes
blossoming, unblossoming into a continuous
inward rain whose levels are the colours
     of pooling while there remains
the unparsed, yet-to-be-parsed, sentence
that runs like water down glass, down trees,
down the channels of vision, into...
     into this and thus, into blasts and clots
of subspeech, unspeech, a speech caught
before it can unblossom into the credible,
which may well be a child at the beginning,
before the detached heavy syllables
of word or phrase or sentence form up into the rhet-
oric of becoming.   It is the gazing at
     slippage, the apprehensions,
the child at its aphabet of breath, the movement
of the mouth, and the rain, the crimson, the time
     lapse. Oh what is it to be thus and thus
and thus depicted, like raindrops, like heavy,
like stepping into the round phrases of rain
that collects at your feet and vanishes.

                                              [GS]

7

Pooling, gravity overrides the flow, settles
in limbs & organs. Striations purple, where
the body decides on verbs. Growing pains
are venous, or bright arterial. So much breath
stored & circulating, ready for articulation.
Stammered out in sleep, among empty rooms
sloughed out, unblossomed. Just get on
with walking, language comes on in rushes,
those first prints. Noisy as similitudes,
overheard on distant radios. Forces favourites,
tuned in to adult ears, or listening in: like drones,
like seersucker, or. Texture of air, adolescent
whoops. Swaying to. Collection, somewhere
circulation stops. Her face is taller than this
room, so much caught. Across in weals, where.
Paint rides up, wants to drive back the ruse
of language, keep to. Dams & foreign flats,
like tides referring to. Continental shelves,
suddenly sucked out to temporary sight.
Neighbourhoods in chance exposure, mouths
are chimneys & vents, they spew & smoke.
In meteoric waters, bacterial whispering.

[CW]

8

Stammered out in sleep, in empty rooms,
words creep up on each other. Someone sleeps
among the pillows, oubliettes and tombs.

Someone is moving silently through deeps
of sleep, past wrecks of continental shelves
where luminous fish explore forgotten heaps

of unused language that must feed themselves.
Someone is awake among the tides. They rise
on all fours where the evidence dissolves.

They break... they stammer. Their open eyes
register the space. They speak as eyes do
in the syntax of moving objects, watchful spies.

Something is falling apart in the beautiful blue
of the impossible sky. Skin. Light. No
common purpose. The child is passing through

the spaces of the mother, crying, O,
O. Of nothing. Of need. Of words. Of this
breakage, this construction of the low

hum, of paint, of pain. We watch words kiss
goodbye to each other. We too go. The rain
is falling without rancour or emphasis.

[GS]

9

Something takes shape. Internal hailing, where
hooks bring rhyme to relief. & landed. Walk

these lines, their fine reverb. Stammering
flick-flacks in the net, where breathing returns

in balance, remains this side of silence, blown
& heaving, elements in play. Unsung, what is

awake. Stirred, red. Unanswered, in sound.
The tricking out of feet, limbed & forgotten

anatomies. Mouth of fish, O. Finds air newly
blistered, where water gives way to travelling

light. Pockets of. Plosive caretaking. Mimicry,
in salt flats, ribbed by retreating. Waters

her face, smooth as drainage. Finds rain without
echo, that point of expansion

suddenly wider. Begin here, set spinning beyond
equivalences. Red stares, sprint out

in paired economies, other pleatings. Pleat this
case. As in some repetition turned bakelite

in the heat, where jets & sprites take off, only
to get the hang of it.

[CW]

10

Truth from the mouths of fish: O O O that
Eliotean rag. *Once upon a time*

in the quest. Quest? I have misheard more
than I ever heard. We live by O O

the misheard *eau* of French water. We duck
and dive out of language into this.

Once upon a time there was a was.
Once upon a time there'll be an is.

Let us make something beautiful out
of water as it streaks and rises.

Let us say 'let us' to the fish of our
complexion. Let us spread our letters

across the surface of the pond and look
to nibble them from beneath. Let the

waves spread out as the fish rise and fall
back into the stony water. Let us

arrange meetings, let us praise and
get the hang of it. Let us repeat after ourselves

this thing that is us, please let us.

[GS]

11

Taken to wild swimming   red finned
& given to *colde welle-stremes   nothynge*

dede   I misheard   each passing cove
as mouthing off   a greener

passage   that stillness   dared in
rocks   readying for   chance

& incapacity   skiffed
where waters   held back from

decision   like marginalia   turned
varicose   marine   it was

already whipping up stormy
kicking on   the waves began

to shoal   refracting   other land
lines   foreign cartilege of   roofs &

tongues   shoreface boundaries
where my feet came down

to rest   is this to repeat after
ourselves   feet in mouths

[CW]

12

On every bow the bryddes herde I synge
Of instruments of strenges in accord
The speech of *fowles* addressed by way of wing
The gulp of fish in air cut by the sword.

Is this then to repeat after ourselves
that foreign cartilage where waves began?
the shoal refracting matters sung by halves?
bryghte creatures summoned by no fisherman?

There's nothing dead that *swymmen* full of *lighte*
the voice that is running away into the space
of speech within the silence that we write
ne herde never, as I gesse

Let us now   break up the stream and allow
skiffed marginalia   let us sing   the *wynd*
there where swetnesse is evermore   enow
to be letting   let each after its kind

prosper. Prosper.

[GS]

13

There's nothing dead that *swymmen*
full of *lighte*　looped &　songed

collateral　scaled up:　silver　runs
through fingers　where corn suggests

another holding　prosperity hulled
in domestic measures　or burned

to bare stubbery　while silver moves in
wilder circulation　grand schools

twitching at predatory inroads　some
disseminate organ readying for least

encounter　where the stream breaks
there might be more than need

I would give you that　vocal start
shoal-shocked　by velocity　harm

seen off in other freight　& life let
go　*of instruments*

[CW]

14

Once they launched out for mackerel
and whiting. The sea was calm. The hooks
attached to the net
> *Lullay lullay*

And so the fish came thriving to the boat
And so the boat filled up with mackerel
And so the boat carried its catch of whiting
> *Lullay*

So silver moves in wider circulation
grand schools and whale roads, so white
so blue. So it runs through fingers
> *Lullay my liking*

This was a tall tale, taller than most.
Stubbery shrubbery, scoffed the late light
mocking and dying under faint high cloud.

[GS]

15

Reach a lull. That you might be rocked
in language, its *blood red roses*. Sounding,
stories. Here is a child, her face large
as houses. Hold to this place of song, *you
pinks & posies*. Her skin was bruised, & *all
in pawn*, waiting for speech, silver & corn.
& still the colour would not arrive,
go down, go down,
shoaled like mackerel across her sight.
& still the land rose up anew
go down, go down,
started up in hammered out blues.
Her red stare caught at this refrain
only to throw it back again.

[CW]

16

This is subsong. It runneth not over
but under. Young birds mumble into air.
They rhyme with each other in the deep
ground bass of language.
          And the child,
she weepeth over not under.
She singeth tears and an archaic
utterance compounded of belly and throat.
We singeth an enormous face
a house with a child at each window.
Waileth. Grievous. This subsong.
Subsonnet. Day not quite ended,
song not quite rounded. Fadeth.
Like a phantom limb. Fadeth.

                                      [GS]

17

Stitch song is wrapped, rhapsodic under
tow. Overheard, low mimicry: *she threw*

the salt cellar at my back, the voices rose
in uncertain dont let me down lyrics, or

sub sounds: a mother & her ripe fruit,
dialects of immeasurable depth hummed

out of thickets. Tell me how it goes, this
time of red mists, chirruped by insects &

resolving like a dew, you'd have me suck.
Walked away, *didn't say a word,*

left her in dense cover, slight fluttering
of throat. Swallowed it.

[CW]

18

Dialects hummed out of thickets. Leaves
sifting sound like tongues. And then the bird
opens its mouth and the child pops out,
a small round call.
          It is all low mimicry,
the *me me* cry slurred. We are all ears,
all hearings   hearing is brightness la la

la

we cram ears with stones & leaves & bird cry
the wind is our politics

we are at the barricades

ripe fruit   red mist

[GS]

19

Might it take this long   to begin
& find silence

makes appointments   still
alongside cargoes of

bright hearing   not yet heard
this morning

the door hinge creaks & swells
after acres of rain

will not shut   speaks of precise
default

[CW]

20

Default into   (space, rain)

and it falls, falls, between spaces into
its default ( ) position. Here.

Just under. And see, cargoes!
Letters, footfall, pacing,
          pressing down on earth
like this   like that

as if water under impact
space   rain   footfall

[GS]

21

I'd think it was her gentle habitat
watching back still roseate

& footfall avoiding recoil   where
space seems empty

she puts her feet down on land
exposures   sheened suddenly

in its draining   her cheek downy
in care   the sun itself

[CW]

22

Sheened, he thought, as of an escape
like a mouth easing into

a smile   sheened, the teeth
clean, swept, as of blossoming

into tongue, palm, plump
something roseate

sudden

[GS]

23

Pink flush of   speech behind
hands   suck-suck

is a fledged bird   stalking
edge of misaligned

doorway   nothing tuneful:
flurried

[CW]

24

Speech is this fledged bird
between the teeth yet flown
into itself.   We have grown
wise in the saying, fledged in the word.

Tuneful. Silent. Savant.

[GS]

25

Refusal comes in atonic
what is the colour I can't say
her cheek bears it   dashed
against   these soundings

[CW]

26

Soundlings   the small cries
you hear in the far distance
settling in the gaps

[GS]

27

What else to take from a mouth's
exception

[CW]

28

You took the words out of my mouth.

[GS]

29

But the struggle to begin, neap tongue

[CW]

30

The tide that sweeps in draws back.
The palm extends, opens then closes.

[GS]

31

Is some fluting desire, set free to slice furrow. Dismayed at converse trouble, held out, assignments of breath.

[CW]

32

Assignments: the breathing, the cold swell
of water in the larynx, of sea, sound of,
breath of, rise of
        and the clear
round mouth of air   wind in a brass bell.

[GS]

33

Rings out, begins again in cool encroachments.
Steps towards the bluff, where trees bend
knowing their flourishing exists to one side
of rising, green banked up by evening, its dark
combs set to forage. Aerial shift of birds.

[CW]

34

And night, and another, as if side by side
and no trees except in the wind,
polite, tapping as if whatever
time continued to measure itself boots
to stride in.   I hear them, and night, and
trees,   as if spoken to, and in, and of.

[GS]

35

Treading night waters, does she wake
in the turn of trees. Threshold value
bringing in the red & yellow, sugared up
waste, sere of words. Damming up
on the line, unable to move for seasonal
smash. Her lip swells with sound, swollen
by decline, the growths of bare branches.

[CW]

36

Red and yellow and not quite, what
was green   the pale and sustain
of light, the back of rain
on streets that open and shut
as a lid opens   and it's dust and fade
and curl, the leaf, the death of it, the rise
of tall grey soundings and mouthings   eyes
focusing in   the year unmade

[GS]

37

Unmaking, where the year's anther gives
up its freight, split to later trust. Small houses
of men and women, their whorls & damp mornings
are fruit & pestle, early buds now heavy in rounded
flesh, its bitter principles. What thread is this
for her to follow, white pith of time catching in a
dry throat, skin suddenly declining & yet scaled
up, as if age arrives in first frosts already melting
to ripe shadow, the nervure of leaves.

[CW]

38

Out into the world, out into the out-of-here
in the sad light, where there are violences...

thus a speech began in the throat and rose
to nowhere, into dead leaves and the suspensions

of rain, small houses, o westron and ever
the west, the runne and the waste, waste

in this hereness and the smale foules
with which we cohabit these red violences,

the opening of blood into leaf, into ground,
the opening suspensions, the rain, the houses.

                                        [GS]

.

39

Caught into the plash of this place,
swerved beyond the time of a child

& into remonstrations, what fricative
stutters out in rainfall   its smallness

rung out in beds, as if fretwork reaches
some distant end. Comfort in declining

light comes on like a swamp, where
pain is dull tension   violence is given

bruise, needs denaturing. Sucked in
as breath is   inhaled & fungiform

you might taste it as she would.

[CW]

40

As she would, the wood of wolverine, the child
with her wolves with her familiar lights of the
imagination scrambling through leaves in dark
December...
    so the child, so the billowing
into the animal orders, the anima analogues,
the mask, the blow-up, the wodeman in his
leaf-lair, leaf-layer, the masks of flowering
into cry...
    so the child flares into darkness
where breast furs, where moths hover
about moons and where houses, houses and walls,
and lengthenings... the days are sliced
into moons, the wolves slanted in the rain.

[GS]

41

Opening a throat to sound, wail of
living kept from the door & finding
entry, she slips out. Is a small bone,
ringing in sharp tongues. The hill,
the afternoon. Darker with the day,
howling at hours, the upcycling
of elements catches her in stir, as
scattered & remade in some later
spring might find in her a storing.
Leaves are lamps, lupine eyes peer
through thickets, adult truths descend
in drones. She has taken the heads
of flowers, arranging headless stems.

[CW]

42

Darker with the day as it moves into...

The voice burnished, strange,

as a bird or dream might be blown through
thickets, as everything grows wildfire
in the neural underground...

and the light lifting, raising of...

wind through the leaves, auburn, bronze,
copper, the speaking voice pitched
to winter, before the stripped branch,
the bare arm gesticulating, seized...
child, child

skin, eye, fingertip, the mind as windswept,
the day as a turning. the night as fur-wrap,

the head delicate, voluminous

[GS]

43

Buried in play, before winter
arrives in quills & sets out its case

rolled up in last resort, stripped
down to heart rot of a peeled twig

sounding of ash, coppiced to
the finality of endings   nilled

sourcings of voice, here she
sends back echoes   where

tunnels & fingertips take you
through the darkness to meet

the sudden purge of light, that
point where it began   to tread

a path, she finds principle
& die-back, diamond

canker, marked out

[CW]

44

Sourcings of voice: window, door, streetlight,
branch scraped and rattled, pod, rain,
wings of wind   so voice, so the sudden

purge

and then nothing, space and nothing, voice
and nothing gaps   here we live in this

in this and that and the winter blanched
unbranched like the sky a white space and grey
and swart and indigo and then and then

so she, child, voice like undersong, heard
through window, door, streetlight, sourcings

of wind and sudden and purge

and this is where this is where voice

breaks and holds its sustaining path,
principle, play, quill, tunnel, ash

[GS]

45

Held spattered debris mounting
past talk past alluvial shakedown
& trials in operational adequacy
walked through: the seasons in
ancestral spaces where sound returns
in afternoon cool & yellow light
in twisted birdsong looped from
hearing not the good of
listening today more a finding
of path willing to set out
in the chill of shadows seeing
her skip ahead a luminous equation
with outlines as if suddenly equal
to skin performance & that voice
her sculptural presence in air
drawn back scalp-tight & redrawn
her standing wave equal to flesh

[CW]

46

Voice as sculpture, the figure standing
in clear ground as a child might stand
in a strong wind before becoming voice

in air, as birdsong, as debris, as face
lost to voice, the song swept far from land
and over, like a mouth on a landing

at the top of, peak of a leaning tower
as it falls, in the earliest November
of its entry with seasons and shadows, the short

fuse of a vanishing that blows apart
only to join here where letter and number
signify the lost precisions, the leaf shower

gone into earth but counted as well as called
by voice, counted on fingers of wind, chill,
the frozen apparatus the iced-up tongue

easing itself from blast into plainsong
and caesura the year at its pivotal
entrance, a voice formed out of cloud

[GS]

47

So much lost. Say she speaks
for the first time now, tells you

in the midst of this bombardment
what it means to begin again,

would mean to begin again
uprooting, before the year

sends out its simulations,
spring heat in prematurity

forcing her out too soon. Is she
a pink bud under glass, so delicate

in her counterbalance with all
the dying, its quiet receding &

detonation. Would she wear
that on her gentle face, as if

her forgetting of return is
present to standing innocence,

already known by it. So that
words come in a pact with living,

now in passage, in setting out.

[CW]

48

See the leaves   what leaves?   the leaves
on the ground, the black hand flapping
the brown hand spread as if to grasp
grasp what?   a paving slab   a street   a sweep
of air   then some cruddy music   and leaf
leaf flattens, is pressed   is what?   is the body
as flat as this as brittle as surrendered   to what?
and some you burn and watch fly   and this
is   what?   an analogy as the mind makes it
of war perhaps   which war? dare we answer? dare
the body be its own dialogue?   dare the
long, shall we say? rain beat down on us
and our music   is that the music?   that cruddy
music you make in your bones and teeth?

who is asking the questions?   there are too
many and late and too soon and this answer
too is a question   only you don't see, no, you
don't hear the question mark − where? − in the leaf
which leaf? that one there, that black-brown-green-
grey thing with its negligible weight, its music.

[GS]

49

Questions shook from latency, where
what splits autumnal takes a turn
for the worse, spores run along a line

in search of energy factories, currencies
for beginning from final ends. Now turned
into sheltered housing, the buildings

that once made shoes & jackboots, still
run through and saturate with labour,
or chance necrosis. Setting in, among

the leaves, this lack of signalling which
comes as full presence, as light dims.
Days pick up ten minutes more, under

cloud, dull pinion. Would you keep warring
from her face, already marked by other
naming, the fakery of seeming negligible,

how lightly words do walk, are spoken.
How the mouth is shaped by movement
forward. Where the tongue is a fish, meeting

air & teeth, the consequence of number.
No surrender but extension of flesh,
handing on. Toothless, liquid, theft.

[CW]

50

Dehiscence, vertigo, time of year, opening
into all possible underworlds that tunnel
under your feet within that shaped mouth,
within that liquid ambience
                    we write
out of lost mouths   extensions of flesh
in winter subways   past the damp
walls of further underworlds   more water,
more wither, more white reckoning, more white
noise running into drains   and so, if there is a so,
move along shoeless, toothless, forward,
through factories, down production lines
that falter   falter and start   and start further back
in rain that soddens and gladdens.
                    It is late
in the season and when she smiles it is
late morning, late in the day, delayed, dying,
suspended, faltering,   light stolen   light fingered,
promethean –
        oh come, come along, now, follow
down tunnels, enter, negotiate, and leave
by the canal past the hurtling water in the mouth,
bearing light, some light, however late, with her
face luminous, liquid, full of tongues, mouths
opening with time of year, vertigo, dehiscence.

[GS]

51

Opens paler at the turn. The year finds
traction & I would stand here. Sidereal
hours, shiny with beginning, call out.
Mouths now dried of sound, landlocked
truths in cracked exposure. Her birth
marks brighter red with winter, face
rising over saturate fens. Tacks
to find direction, warmth of breath,
where blood rises to this surface.
What comes up to test in other
elemental scores, eyes of catfish
unaccustomed to new light, poke
the slowest subterranean gangways.
Heads & whiskers. Rheumy flesh
turns up, readying to regroup. Thick as
days. Their yellow rind, shed. And hers
venturing out, untempered, soft to what
is deathless in arrival, time bent in.
Movement towards summer, while.
On her face it spreads, takes flight, or.
Flocks towards care, roosting seconds.
Waiting on boughs until the day gives,
shadows keeping agile, accounting.

[CW]

52

Sunblown, unseasonal, the year's breath stopped
for an instant, unsteady yet breathing, light
of a billowing. Look, leaves, hurl themselves
into small storms, the light dripping off them
like rain. Where are we, she, her mouth, the dry
season of mouths? Crow, blackbird, rook
caw breath, croak into dry trees. And then rain
slithering down bark, blurting its glut
and overflow.
    There is no arriving here, no here
except this prism between the narrowest
of narrow through which sound escapes, flirts
with meaning then stops short. The words
slip through sidereal space, each black hole
an eyelet, a blackbird's call, a boxwood flute,
a chook, a slippage, an inside-out.
                      Unseasonal
birth-mark, red and rising, re-rising, the day
with its red sun to begin and end with...

... as if voice could turn itself out or become
whistle, swoop, alarm – chook, chook – as swift
as a sidereal moment within which the universe
were concentrated, like juice, like rain, as
sunblown as this mouth, this catfish, this
perfunctory closeness, prefunct, profruct
prefict, purrfruck, prelimary, fragile.

                                          [GS]

53

Sunblown, refusing liking, in the name of things. Or touch. Where voice is rooked out of time, always the generational push. Force & hurling air, quiet turbulence of mornings. Sinecure of eyelids, go on doing that work, & the heart. Is wilder than you would guess, missing its cue here & there. Colour inarticulate, flushing through sluices unnoticed. No resignation in her look, but fast forwarding of flutes & eyelets, each a rung beat, each a mystery & flocking to resolve in answering faces. Wheezing rivers recover in instants, the smallest green testing how to rise, given the outlook on trust. Would it thrust this way. Her face a large moon, determining what is broadcast to herself, allowing joy at distance, deep in forests never experienced, scent of. Dark pine, the sweat & oil of years airborne, pheromone call to. What might never be, the bonds of hours, holding. Are never perfunctory, stronger than anyone owns. Snagged beneath the eyes, a red start reflecting elsewhere, rosiness woken again from sleep, that drainage of fens.

[CW]

54

As if woken from sleep or if not from sleep
from something resembling sleep, where the eyes
are closed and the breath even and full, as at times
of genuine calm, such as you need in order
to enter the sleep from which you will wake
at the manifest hour, after the requisite space
of unconsciousness, corridors, elephants,
and the deep scent of something unnameable
poignant and lost, like any awakening
into the light filtered through the eye
with its faint pillowed lid that vibrates
only according to its own laws of sleep
and awakening, as if woken from, as if.

Her face a large moon. Dark pine. Awakening.
Red start. Hurling air. Wings dipped. Fallen.
The moon still larger. The pine still dark.
As dark as before. But lighter. Rook. Wood.
Sluice. Stop and stop. Stop. And the waking.
And stop. And sweat. And oil. Flutes. Eyelets.
Stop. The rivers. The broadcast. And stopping.
The moon dark and large, Awakening.
Larger. Its full sweaty face. Burned by it.
Burned by the moon. And stop. Sweat. Lighter.
Leaf. Sluice. Is wilder. Stop. And a gust.
Stop. Corridor. Pillow and elephant. And stop.
And stop. And wake. And stop. And stop.

[GS]

55

That drainage, its winter pelt. Is there
doughed up painterly. Have her breathe,
where the frame slips out, already on the
move. Stepping simultaneous, words are
brink, they shell. Out, the residues of tides,
concert of fishes, the twitch of grander
masses. Held & not held, falling from laps
& skirts to watch the impress of her own
feet. This colour, what is it. Tending, where
fibre is the tougher for the hurt. I call her
cicatrice, the opening thick with morning.
Bound into intimations of sleet, this moment,
colder fronts, yet hearing. Something bound,
meaning. More than attachment, the leap
that sends her running among the red dunes.
Rubble, bare branches, a clarity of lines &
edges where her eye rests. Those iris crypts.
All returning as flesh, where her head wishes
to turn, & does, while the face remains. Caught
in lags, stayed by. What is active or quiet, these
gaps are never still, small building spaces, for
switch of consequence, or pacing. Towards
the place of speech, its overspill. Or harmful
fascinations, where. Skin takes over the task
of telling, its folds & scrimping. In light,
the action of. Continual beginning. It stops,
& then. Colours return, start, move on.

[CW]

56

So we. And move on. Everything disappears
in that cold residue. It's getting late
for the mouth and its burned tide, for the frame
that mouths and languages accumulate.

Late, and the twitch and step, the mournings
of the branches as they work through the system,
running among red dunes in the place of speech
and its overspill. The wild mouths. We know them.

*

Now we are at removes. Out in the street
an elderly woman. A child ducks out of an alley.
The shop with its lights and frame. It is
the intimate tide. Nights in with the family.

But it breaks, just as mouths break, as lines
break in the moving, as the residue, the dew
bright in the mouth, stops, and we move on.
The eye rests. The tongue flows through

the tide. Here the scrimmage, the fishes thrust
in droves flicking past towards the place
of speech which is here / not here in streams
of gibberish and gladrush and glyphgrace.

*

She moves among rubble and bare. The face
breaks with the tide, the mouth in the core,
on its course, in its heartdrive. We speak and scrimp.
Could we begin again it would not be here

but another hearing and hearting. The fish
scamper, the face addresses the tongue. It's late
and the wind is caught in the mouth of the clock.
Bare branches. Clarities. The clear cold night.

[GS]

BIOGRAPHICAL NOTES

GEORGE SZIRTES was born in Hungary in 1948 and came to England as a refugee in 1956. Having studied Fine Art, he published his first book of poems, *The Slant Door*, in 1979. It won the Faber Memorial Prize. He has published many since then, winning the T S Eliot Prize for *Reel* in 2004, and was shortlisted for the same prize for his two subsequent books, *The Burning of the Books* (2009) and *Bad Machine* (2013). His *New and Collected Poems* appeared in 2008.

He is also a prize-winning translator of poetry and fiction from Hungarian.

CAROL WATTS was born in the Midlands in 1962. At 11 she came to London to meet Stephen Spender, who awarded her a prize in the 3M National Poetry Competition. She stopped writing in her early 20s, returning to poetry two decades later. Her work includes *Wrack* (2007), *Occasionals* (2011), *Mother Blake* (2012), *Sundog* (2013) and *Many Weathers Wildly Comes* (2015). A series of pamphlets *When Blue Light Falls* is due shortly in a single volume. A professor of literature and poetics, she often performs and works collaboratively across media, and in the form of artists' books.

Selected titles in Arc Publications'
POETRY FROM THE UK / IRELAND include:

D. M. BLACK
Claiming Kindred

JAMES BYRNE
Blood / Sugar
White Coins

DONALD ATKINSON
In Waterlight:
Poems New, Selected & Revised

JOANNA BOULTER
Twenty Four Preludes & Fugues on
Dmitri Shostakovich

TONY CURTIS
What Darkness Covers
The Well in the Rain
folk
Approximately in the Key of C

JULIA DARLING
Indelible, Miraculous
COLLECTED POEMS

LINDA FRANCE
You are Her
Reading the Flowers

KATHERINE GALLAGHER
Circus-Apprentice
Carnival Edge

CHRISSIE GITTINS
Armature

RICHARD GWYN
Sad Giraffe Café

GLYN HUGHES
A Year in the Bull-Box

MICHAEL HASLAM
The Music Laid Her Songs in Language
A Sinner Saved by Grace
A Cure for Woodness

MICHAEL HULSE
The Secret History
Half-Life

CHRISTOPHER JAMES
Farewell to the Earth

BRIAN JOHNSTONE
The Book of Belongings
Dry Stone Work

JOEL LANE
Trouble in the Heartland
The Autumn Myth

HERBERT LOMAS
The Vale of Todmorden
A Casual Knack of Living
COLLECTED POEMS

SOPHIE MAYER
(O)

PETE MORGAN
August Light

MICHAEL O'NEILL
Wheel
Gangs of Shadow

MARY O'DONNELL
The Ark Builders
Those April Fevers

IAN POPLE
An Occasional Lean-to
Saving Spaces

JOS SMITH
Subterranea

PAUL STUBBS
The Icon Maker
The End of the Trial of Man

LORNA THORPE
A Ghost in My House
Sweet Torture of Breathing

ROISIN TIERNEY
The Spanish-Italian Border

MICHELENE WANDOR
Musica Transalpina
Music of the Prophets
Natural Chemistry

JACKIE WILLS
Fever Tree
Commandments
Woman's Head as Jug